D1402124

The Seven Continents

South America

by Karen Bush Gibson

Consultant:
Mark Healy
Professor of Geography
William Rainey Harper College
Palatine, Illinois

Capstone press

Mankato, Minnesota

Bridgestone Books are published by Capstone Press,
151 Good Counsel Drive, P.O. Box 669, Mankato, Minnesota 56002.
www.capstonepress.com

Library of Congress Cataloging-in-Publication Data
Gibson, Karen Bush.
    South America / Karen Bush Gibson.
      p. cm.—(Bridgestone books. The seven continents)
      Summary: "Describes the continent of South America, including climate, landforms, plants,
animals, countries, people, as well as South America and the world"—Provided by publisher.
      Includes bibliographical references and index.
      ISBN-13: 978-0-7368-5431-3 (hardcover)
      ISBN-10: 0-7368-5431-2 (hardcover)
      1. South America—Juvenile literature. 2. South America—Geography—Juvenile literature. I. Title.
II. Series: Seven continents (Mankato, Minn.)
F2208.5.G53 2006
980—dc22   2005018053

Editorial Credits
Becky Viaene, editor; Patrick D. Dentinger, designer; Kim Brown and Tami Collins, map illustrators;
    Wanda Winch, photo researcher; Scott Thoms, photo editor

Photo Credits
Brand X Pictures/Philip Coblentz, 12 (bottom right); Digital Vision Ltd./Gerry Ellis, 12 (left);
Map Resources, cover (background); Minden Pictures/Frans Lanting, cover (foreground); Peter Arnold,
Inc./John Maier, 18 (top); Photodisc/Sexto Sol/Ernesto Rios Lanz, 1; South American Pictures/Chris
Sharp, 6 (top); South American Pictures/Tony Morrison, 6 (bottom, both), 10 (both), 12 (top right),
16, 18 (bottom); South American Pictures/Steve Bowles, 20

1 2 3 4 5 6 11 10 09 08 07 06

Table of Contents

Continents of the World

South America

  South America is a continent of contrasts. Major **climate** differences are found on its 6,888,706 square miles (17,821,029 square kilometers). This landmass has some of the world's wettest and driest areas. **Rain forests** in Choco, Colombia, get rain almost every day. In Chile's Atacama **Desert**, it may rain only three times in 100 years.

  Contrasts also exist among the people. From large cities to small villages, mansions to cardboard shacks, variety is part of daily life on this continent.

◄ South America is the fourth largest continent. It is connected to North America.

Climate

South America is well-known for the tropical climate of its rain forests. These forests cover much of the northern part of the continent.

A variety of climates make up the rest of South America. Dry grasslands border the rain forests and cover much of the continent's southern half. The hot Atacama Desert lies along the western coast. Towering above all is the cold mountain climate of the Andes. High in the Andes, temperatures rarely rise above freezing.

◄ South America's climates include wet, plant-covered rain forests, dry deserts, and snow-covered mountains.

Landforms of SOUTH AMERICA

NORTH AMERICA

CARIBBEAN SEA

Magdalena River

Orinoco River

GUIANA HIGHLANDS

Negro River

Branco River

Japura River

Amazon River

Amazon River

AMAZON RAIN FOREST REGION

Marañon River

Yavari River

Purus River

Madeira River

Tapajós River

Araguaia River

Tocantins River

Sao Francisco River

Ucayali River

A N D E S   M O U N T A I N S

BRAZILIAN HIGHLANDS

Pilcomayo River

Paraná River

ATACAMA DESERT

Salado River

Paraná River

Uruguay River

PACIFIC OCEAN

ATLANTIC OCEAN

▲ Mount Aconcagua
22,834 feet
(6,959 meters)

PAMPAS

LEGEND
▲ Highest point
▦ Mountains
⌒ River

N
W   E
S

0 200 400 600 800 1000 Kilometers

0   200   400   600 Miles

8

Landforms

The Andes Mountains stretch along South America's west coast. The Andes are the world's longest mountain range.

Many rivers, including the Marañón and Ucayali, start in the Andes. These rivers form the world's largest river, the Amazon. This river flows east in the Amazon rain forest.

Below the Amazon rain forest dry plains, called Pampas, cover part of the continent's south half. South America's driest area, the Atacama Desert, is northwest of these plains.

Plants

Thousands of plants grow only in South America's Amazon rain forest. Medicine made from the Amazon's cinchona tree helps treat **malaria**.

Near the rain forest, farmers grow coffee plants and cacao trees. Beans from cacao trees are used to make chocolate.

Few plants grow in the Atacama Desert or high on the snow-covered Andes Mountains. Only grass and other tough plants can grow in the harsh climates of these areas.

◄ The Amazon rain forest has a wide variety of plants. Few plants grow on the Atacama Desert's dry land.

Animals

Around 25 percent of the world's animal **species** live in South America. The largest variety of animals lives in the Amazon rain forest. Colorful birds, giant snakes, and billions of insects make homes in this forest.

Near the rain forest, hungry animals find food on the grasslands. Jaguars dart across the land to catch tapirs. Flightless birds, called rheas, munch on plants.

In the cold Andes Mountains, thick fur keeps animals warm. Alpacas, llamas, and tiny **chinchillas** survive in this cold climate.

◄ A macaw eats fruit from rain forest trees. A tapir cools off in a river (top right). Thick fur keeps a llama warm.

Countries of South America

NORTH AMERICA

Caribbean Sea

VENEZUELA

GUYANA

SURINAME

FRENCH GUIANA (France)

COLOMBIA

GALAPAGOS ISLANDS (ECUADOR)

ECUADOR

BRAZIL

PERU

PACIFIC OCEAN

BOLIVIA

CHILE

PARAGUAY

Kilometers
0   500   1000

0   620
Miles

URUGUAY

ARGENTINA

ATLANTIC OCEAN

N
W   E
S

FALKLAND ISLANDS (UNITED KINGDOM)

SOUTH GEORGIA (UNITED KINGDOM)

Countries

South America is made up of 12 countries and three **territories**. The country of Brazil covers almost half of the continent. It is almost as big as the United States. Brazil also has South America's largest population. More than 180 million people live in Brazil.

South America's largest city is also in Brazil. São Paulo is home to more than 18 million people. Millions of people also live in Lima, Peru, Rio de Janeiro, Brazil, and Buenos Aires, Argentina.

Population Density of South America

People per square mile		People per square kilometer
Less than 2		Less than 1
2 to 25		1 to 10
25 to 125		10 to 50
125 to 250		50 to 100
More than 250		More than 100

● Major Cities/Urban Centers
More than 7.5 million people

People

About 365 million people live in South America. More than 75 percent live and work in crowded cities along the coasts. The rest live in small villages and work on farms.

Hundreds of different languages are spoken in South America. Spanish is the main language in most countries. Millions of people also speak Portuguese.

Nearly all South Americans have the same religion. About 90 percent are Roman Catholic. Others are Protestant, Buddhist, and Jewish.

◄ The amount of education South American children get depends on where they live and their family's income.

Living in South America

South America's poor and wealthy have very different houses. Wealthy people live in large houses, while millions of poor people live in favelas. In these slums, people live in homes made of cardboard and metal scraps.

Many South Americans wear **modern** clothing. Quechua people living high in the cold Andes Mountains bundle in warm **traditional** clothing.

South Americans enjoy a variety of foods. Beef, beans, and fruit are part of most meals. Coffee is a common drink.

◀ Millions of poor South Americans live in favelas (top). Few can afford large, expensive houses.

South America and the World

One of the world's greatest resources is South America's Amazon rain forest. It is the largest rain forest in the world. More than half of all plant and animal species come from the world's rain forests.

Rain forest plants help the environment by soaking up harmful carbon dioxide. Rain forests, including the Amazon, also provide many people with medicine and food. Worldwide, people realize the importance of South America's Amazon rain forest and are working to study and protect it.

◄ In a South American rain forest, a scientist uses a net to catch and study butterflies.

Glossary

chinchilla (chin-CHIL-uh)—a small South American rodent

climate (KLYE-mit)—the usual weather in a place

desert (DEZ-urt)—a very dry area of land; deserts receive less than 10 inches (25 centimeters) of rain each year.

malaria (muh-LAIR-ee-ah)—a serious disease that people get from mosquito bites

modern (MOD-urn)—up-to-date or new in style

rain forest (RAYN FOR-ist)—a tropical forest where much rain falls

species (SPEE-sheez)—a group of animals with similar features; members of a species can mate and produce young.

territory (TER-uh-tor-ee)—land under the control of a country

traditional (truh-DISH-uhn-uhl)—the styles, manners, and ways of the past

Read More

Sayre, April Pulley. *South America, Surprise!* Our Amazing Continents. Brookfield, Conn.: Millbrook Press, 2003.

Striveildi, Cheryl. *South America.* A Buddy Book. Edina, Minn.: Abdo, 2003.

Internet Sites

FactHound offers a safe, fun way to find Internet sites related to this book. All of the sites on FactHound have been researched by our staff.

Here's how:
1. Visit *www.facthound.com*
2. Type in this special code **0736854312** for age-appropriate sites. Or enter a search word related to this book for a more general search.
3. Click on the **Fetch It** button.

FactHound will fetch the best sites for you!

Index